MUCH ADO
ABOUT
STUFFING

MUCH ADO ABOUT STUFFING

THE BEST AND WORST OF

@CrapTaxidermy

ADAM R. S. CORNISH

Andrews McMeel
Publishing

Kansas City • Sydney • London

". . . and for my next trick, I, the Amazing Ferreto, am going to disappear up your trouser leg and make you dance uncontrollably."

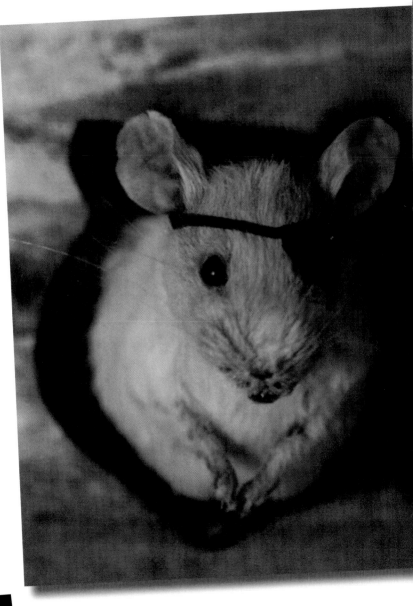

"So I welcomed them to Woodbury;
what a mistake that was.
They killed my daughter, stabbed me
in the eye, and to top it off,
one of them left a skid mark
on my toilet."

"Would you like
a souvenir photo
from your ride on
Splash Mountain?"

". . . and I said to him, 'Derek! I know there aren't many job opportunities for raccoons at the moment, but you need to do something. We can't eat out of bins forever.'"

"Elaine! I am absolutely fuming—I only went for a filling and this is what he did to my teeth! The guys at work have started calling me fucking Molar Bear!"

"I'm sorry, Alan, but if you insist on sleeping under cars this was bound to happen at some point."

"Winning that ticket, Squirrel Rose, was the best thing that ever happened to me; it brought me to you."

"Oh, fuck. The missus is going to kill me when I tell her I lost our nest under the floorboards."

"Jesse. We need to cook."

"You've got to see the positives in life, Steve. You could say that you are missing a horn. I say you became a unicorn."

23

"Please can we go to McDonald's, Daddy? Please!"

"Heck, I'm real nervous, so I'm just gonna go ahead and say it. Paula Prickly, will you go to the dance with me?"

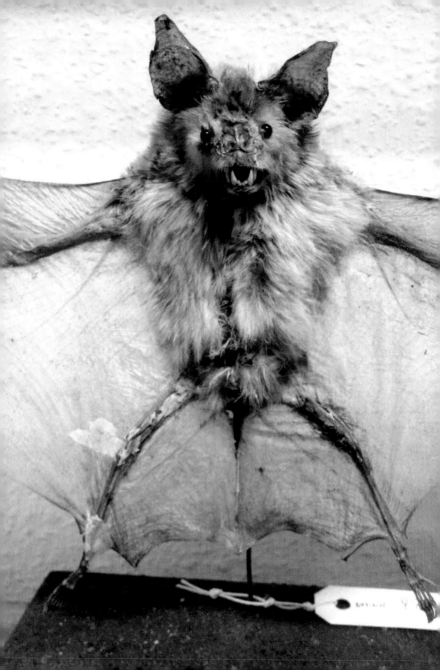

"I'm sorry to disappoint you, Daddy, but I'm far too fabulous to play football. I was born to dance!"

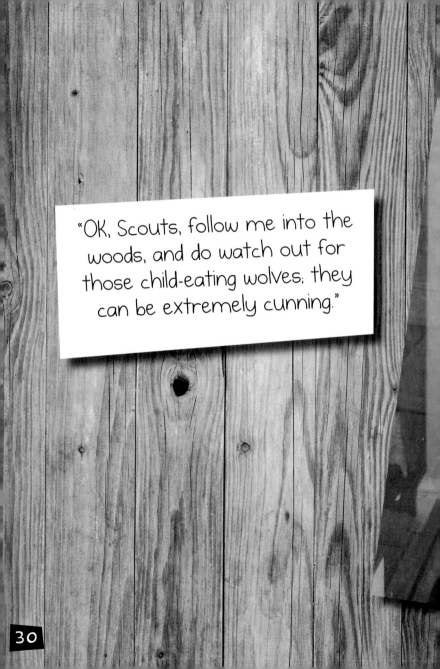

"OK, Scouts, follow me into the woods, and do watch out for those child-eating wolves; they can be extremely cunning."

"Hey, I just met you, and this is crazy. But please come closer; your arms look tasty."

"Look, Sasha, I've been building dams all frickin' day. If I want a beer, I'll have a beer. Get off my case, woman."

"It's not fair; I don't want to go to bed! Simon Spottyface's parents let him stay up until 10:30 on school nights!"

"Look, Princess, I just don't think that Prince Ali guy is good enough for you. I mean, he said he was going to show you the world but he just flew you around the block like twice on an old carpet."

"After we finished filming *Star Wars*, the work just kinda stopped. Like one minute you're piloting the Millennium Falcon shooting Storm Troopers and shit, the next you can't even get a walk-on part in a daytime soap. It got so bad I had to pawn my silver chest belt thing to pay my rent one month. I couldn't handle it, man; it turned me to drink. Every day I would open a bottle, sit by the phone, and wait for it to ring. Sometimes I'd try to call Harrison, but the guy just didn't want to know. It's when you're at your lowest that you realize who your real friends are. I can't say it wasn't a tough time, but thankfully those dark days are behind me. I've been dry for two years now and with the help of Wookie Jesus I intend to keep it that way."

"Margaret! I've got to give a PowerPoint presentation to the board today. Where the fuck have you put my toupee?!"

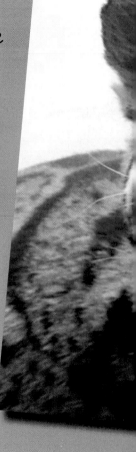

"What's that, Lassie? Little Timmy has fallen down the old wishing well and you're too fabulous to care?!"

"Take my strong hand, child."

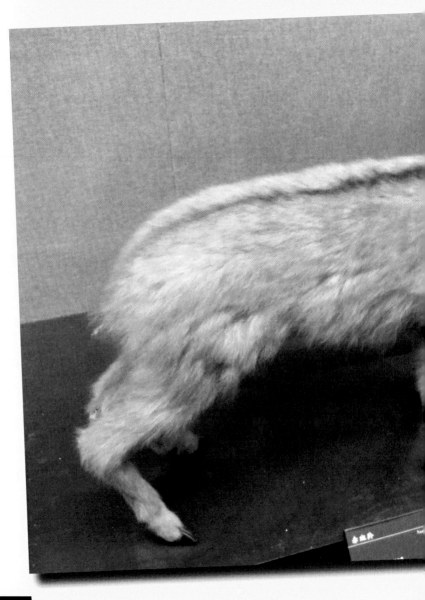

That moment when you hear someone talking behind your back ...

"'No, Colin, I've looked at the forecast; you won't need an umbrella today,' she says!"

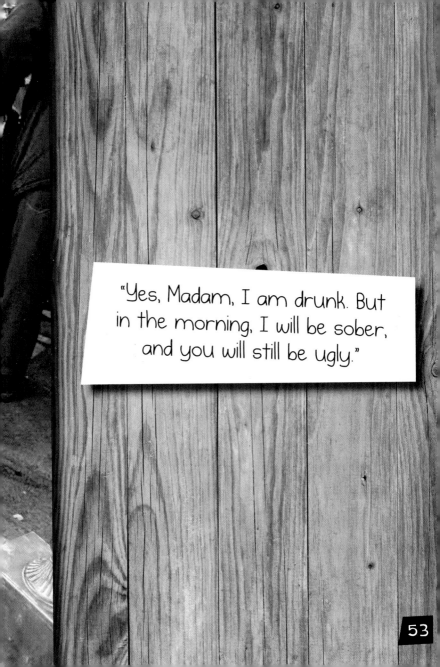

"Yes, Madam, I am drunk. But in the morning, I will be sober, and you will still be ugly."

"I'm telling you, Mike, the best way to prevent a hangover is just to not stop drinking."

That awkward moment when
the beat never drops . . .

"Don't worry, Grandma, we'll have a nice family photo when Charlie's finished messing around."

"I'm telling you, Julia, it's a good thing
I've got bloody sonar because
they've made a right mess of
my laser eye surgery!"

ers live in woodland, feeding on almost
hey find from worms and fr...
Whole families...

"Draw me like one of your French girls."

"Lauren. We need to leave.
I think I've just sharted myself."

"Think, Patty, think.
Did I leave the oven on?"

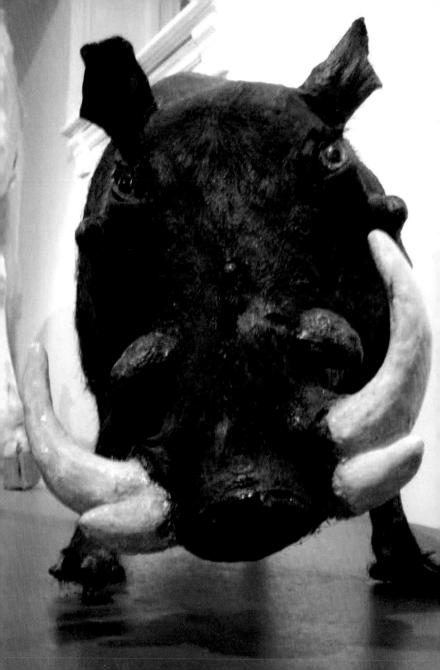

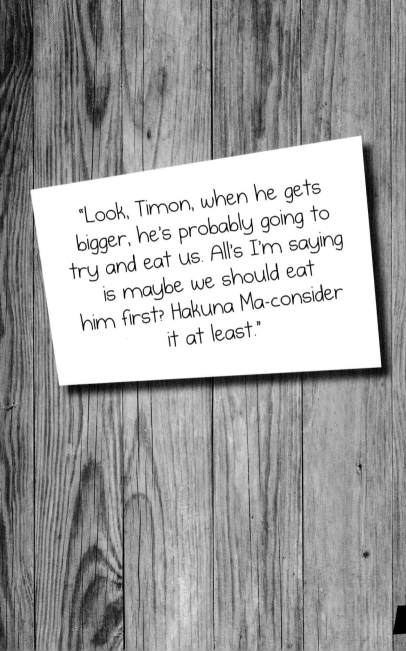

"Look, Timon, when he gets bigger, he's probably going to try and eat us. All's I'm saying is maybe we should eat him first? Hakuna Ma-consider it at least."

"I am never drinking again."

"Hey guys, glad you're home.
Somebody left a half-eaten zebra in
the living room and took a
shit on the couch."

"Cirque du Soleil
ain't got shit on Barry!"

"It's called fashion, darling.
Look it up sometime."

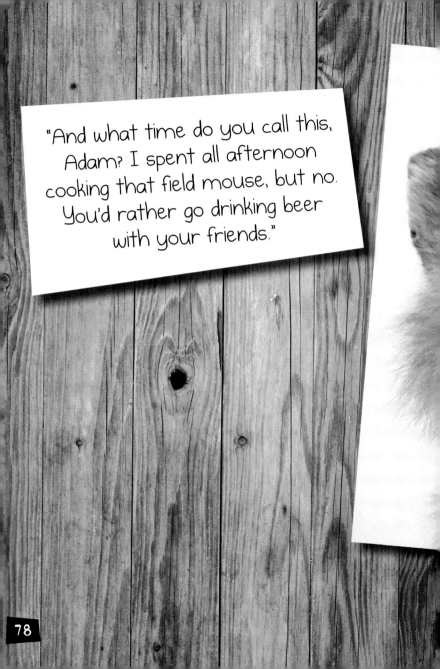

"And what time do you call this, Adam? I spent all afternoon cooking that field mouse, but no. You'd rather go drinking beer with your friends."

"Yeah, Mr. White. Yeah, Science!"

"'Go to your room, Charlie.
Don't spoil family photos, Charlie.
You're grounded, Charlie.'
God I hate this. I'm gonna run
away from home; then they'll
be sorry."

"You must be joking, darling, we haven't eaten free-range mice since Roger got his promotion."

"You talkin' to me?
Then who the hell else are
you talkin' to? You talkin' to
me? Well, I'm the only one
here. Who the fox do you
think you're talking to?"

"Damn girl, you lookin' fiiiiine.
You get my seal of approval."

"Who's awesome? That's right,
buddy, you are."

"What does the fox say?
Well, for starters, may
I request a more ergonomic chair?
This one is playing havoc with
my posture."

I'll level with you all.

This being my first book, I wasn't sure what to expect. The process was alien to me and, in all honesty, an emotional roller-coaster ridden by anatomically incorrect, dead animals.

That said, there are certain people who helped me through it, and I hope by mentioning them here they might forgive me if I was a dick to them:

Mum and Dad, Lauren, Sasha (not sure how you helped but I knew you'd be a dick if I didn't include you), Patty and Andrews McMeel (for recognizing talent when they see it), all my Twitter followers, Alan White and Buzzfeed, Adele, Kat, Nyla, @UnnamedInsider, Ry and Laura (this mention counts as your wedding present), Carli and Dan, @Elequenoaporta, @TheBlogess, Steve and Becky, good Rat, Cone, Nick, AJ, Vegas Child (the greatest band you've never heard of), @ScouseGirlProblems, Mary from Coronation Street, Maia Dunphy and Johnny Vegas, Jeremy Vine, Gemma Anne Styles, Klaxons, Jeremy Clarkson, Har Mar Superstar, David Flatman, @_YouHadOneJob, Joel and everyone at Unite, all my mates, the Royal FC, and Sheffield Wednesday. (If I've missed anyone, I'll buy you a pint to say sorry.)

Photo credits:
@XTCJesus, Chris Constantine, Linden Tea, Timothy Medhurst, Colin Ingram, @Joe_Nash1 and @KlWhite1985, Jellibat, Denise Brereton, @kevinliddell4, Siv Osterlund, Matt Rudge, Ellen Rose, Conrad Gillet, Wikipedia user Daderot, Navreet Chawla, David Morris, Julie Dermansky, @NocombRick, Shaena A Montanari, James Stewart, Clare Racey, @Famron, Ellie May, Emily Oldfield, and Katrina Villa Herman.

Special thanks:

Adele Morse is an ethical taxidermist and made Geoff (the fox from the cover), the Amazing Ferreto, and Governor Rat. She is fucking awesome at it and teaches classes; for more info, go to AdeleMorseTaxidermy.co.uk.

Sarah Burhouse is an ethical taxidermist/poor student who made the fantastic Heisenberg and Jesse Rats, both of which are available to buy from her store: etsy.com/uk/shop/Snailsales.

Jeremy Johnson is an ethical taxidermist and made the incredible Barry the Badger and the Raccoon Family. Check out more of his work over at MeddlingWithNature.com.

Tony Dunnell is a photographer/blogger who has posted some outstanding pictures and articles. Find them at HowToPeru.com.

Also, thank you for buying the book. With every purchase, not only are you lining my pockets but also a donation will be made to help care for some living animals over at Thornberry Animal Sanctuary in South Yorkshire, United Kingdom.

Nish

Andrews McMeel Publishing, LLC
an Andrews McMeel Universal company
1130 Walnut Street, Kansas City, Missouri 64106

www.andrewsmcmeel.com

14 15 16 17 18 RR2 10 9 8 7 6 5 4 3 2 1

ISBN: 978-1-4494-6328-1

Library of Congress Control Number: 2014941953

Editor: Patty Rice
Art director: Tim Lynch
Production manager: Cliff Koehler
Production editor: Erika Kuster
Demand planner: Sue Eikos